PHILOSOPHICAL QUOTES OF GREAT MEN

JONATHAN IKECHUKWU WILLIE

PREFACE

Man exists in a universe of complex ideologies that motivates our actions, principles, ethical values, and dialectical views. These in effects gears him for an inner feeling based on actualizing his dreams. To harness these resources, he has to propagate theories or hypotheses to guide him in a world where we are faced with saturated and complex ideologies.

To visualize our inner objectives, words have become the chemical components mixed to express our desired objectives. Therefore, I have selected these major chemical components as expressed by various individuals through history to foster such harmony in our mutual development in terms of speech production.

This book will further strengthen and bringing these quotes to our present-day limelight and reality. These witty or humorous sayings contain the factual that lubricates our discussions or speeches. It will give added flavor in our day-to-day discussions and will be the essence of motivational speakers wired to direct their thoughts.

This book discoursed a way and the desire to galvanize the intricacies in public speech presentation. This book will guide and direct those in public gatherings to present a well-lubricated polished speech, that will receive several applauds of the listener both in oral and written presentations.

Our daily discussions without references to these famous quotes will be like a nice food without necessary spices.

These famous quotes remind us of great and treacherous past. These are quotes that made our history and will serve as our guide into our future.

"These famous speeches lifted heart in dark times, gave hope in despair, refined the

character of men, inspired brave feats, gave courage to the weary, honored the dead and changed the course of history. It is my desire that this library will become a lasting resource not only to those who wish to become great orators but to all men who wisely seek out the great mentor of history as guides on the path to virtuous manhood".

Life is a gift that has been given to you. It is in your hands to make the best out of it--dare to believe that you can. Through the ups and downs, you'll find a lesson to learn that will make you a better person. Each experience-- good and bad--makes you grow. Get along with life and surely, things will become easier for you. Live for today and enjoy every moment. Capture the best that life has to offer you.

DEDICATION

This book is dedicated to the Highest, Most Merciful, Most Mighty, the Everlasting Creator and Ruler of the Universe, the Ancient of days. Omnipresent and Omniscience God and to all my children and grandchildren.

Table of Contents

PREFACE..2
DEDICATION.....................................5
CHAPTER ONE................................21
   ABILITY...21
   ACCOMPLISHMENT 21
   ACTION 21
   ADVERSITY 22
   ADVICE...22
   AFRAID 22
   AGREEMENT 22
   AMBITION...22
   ANARCHISM...27
   ANGER 27
   APRON 28
   ARGUMENTS...28
   ART 28
   ARTIST..29
   ATTITUDE...29
   ATTENTION..29

CHAPTER TWO..............................30

BACHELOR..30

BALLOT...30

BEAUTY 30

BELIEVE 30

BEST 31

BIBLE 31

BIRTH 31

BLACK MAN...31

BLESSING 32

BOLDNESS...32

BOOKS..32

BRAVERY 32

BURDEN 33

BUREAUCRACY...33

BUSY...34

CHAPTER THREE...........................35

CHAGRIN...35

CHALLENGE...35

CHANGE 36

CHARACTER 37

CHARITY 37

CHASE 37

CHILD 37

CHILDREN 38

CHRISTIANITY...39

CITIZEN 39

COLOR...40

COMMITMENT 40

COMMUNICATION..40

CONFLICTS 40

CONSCIENCE 41

CONSOLATION 41

CONSEQUENCES 41

CONTEMPT 41

CONTRADICTION 41

CORRUPTION 42

COURAGE...42

COWARD..43

CREATIVITY 43

CREDITOR 43

CROWD 43

CRY..43

CHAPTER FOUR............................44

DANCE 44
DEAD 44
DEBT 45
DECISION 45
DEMOCRACY 45
DESIRE 46
DESPAIR 46
DESTINATION 46
DESTINY 46
DETERMINATION 46
DIFFICULTY 47
DISAPPOINTMENT 48
DISCIPLINE 48
DISCOURAGEMENT 48
DISCOVERY 48
DISTRACTION 49
DOUBT 49
DREAM 49

CHAPTER FIVE 51

ECONOMY 51
EDUCATION 51
ELDER 51

9

ELECTION 51

EMOTION 52

ENEMY 52

ENDURANCE 52

ENGLAND 52

ENVIRONMENT 53

EQUALITY 53

EQUITY 53

EUROPE 53

EVIL 53

EXCLUSION 54

EXCELLENCE 54

CHAPTER SIX 55

FAITH 55

FALSEHOOD 55

FAME 55

FAMILY 55

FATE 55

FEAR 56

FLATTER 56

FOCUS 56

FOOLS 56

FOOTPRINT 57

FORGIVENESS... 57

FRIENDS 57

FRUSTRATION 57

FULFILLMENT 58

CHAPTER SEVEN 59

GAIN 59

GIFT 59

GIRLS 59

GIVING 59

GOALS 59

GOD 60

GOOD 61

GOOD PERSON 61

GOVLRNANCE 62

GREATEST 62

GROWTH 63

CHAPTER EIGHT 64

HAPPINESS 64

HARMONY 65

HATE 65

HEALTH 65

HEART 65

HOLD ON...66

HONESTY 66

Honor 66

HOPE 66

HUMBLE 67

CHAPTER NINE 68

IDEA 68

IMMORALITY 68

IMPERIALISM 68

IMPOSITION 68

IMPOSSIBILITY 69

INCOMPETENCY 69

INDEPENDENCE 69

INFALLIBLE 69

INFERIORITY...69

INDULGENCE 70

INJUSTICE 70

INNOCENT 70

INSPIRATION...70

INSANE..70

INTEGRITY 71

INTELLECTUAL	71
INTENTION	71

CHAPTER TEN 71

JOURNEY	72
JUSTICES	72

CHAPTER ELVEN 73

KIND WORDS	73
KINGDOM	73
KNOWLEDGE	73

CHAPTER TWELVE 75

LANGUAGE	75
LAW	75

Kenneth Kaunda 75

LAZZY	76
LEADERSHIP	76
LEARN	77
LEGACY	77
LESSON	78
LIFE	78
LIFE'S THEORY	82
LIBERALS	87

LIGHT 88

LITERACY 88

LITERATURE 88

LIVING 89

LONELINESS 89

LOVE 89

CHAPTER THIRTEEN 91

MADNESS 91

MAN 91

MANIPULATION 92

MARRIAGE 92

MAJORITY 93

MASSES 93

MEDIA 93

MEETING 93

MEMORANDUM 93

MEMORIES 94

MEN 94

MERIT 94

MISSION 94

MISTAKE 94

MIRACLES 95

MISERABLE 95
MONEY 95
MOTION 96
MOTIVATION 96
MUSIC 96

CHAPTER FOURTEEN 97

NATURE 97
NECESSITY 97
NOTHING 97

CHAPTER FIFTEEN 98

OLD 98
OLD AGE 98
OPINION 99
OPPORTUNITY 99
OBSTINATE 99
OPPRESSION 99
OPTIMISM 99

CHAPTER SIXTEEN 100

PARADISE 100
PARTNER 100
PEOPLE 100
PERFECTION 101

Henry Wadsworth Longfellow 101

- PLAN 101
- POLICEMEN 102
- POLITICS 102
- POSITIVE 103
- POSSIBILITY 103
- POSTULATIONS 104
- POTENTIAL 104
- POWER 104
- PRACTICE 105
- PRAYER 105
- PRETENSE 106
- PRINCIPLES 106
- PRIVILEGE 106
- PROBLEMS 107

CHAPTER SEVENTEEN 109

- QUESTION 109

CHAPTER EIGHTEEN 110

- RACISM 110
- RECKLESSNESS 110
- RELATIONSHIP 110
- REMEMBRANCE 111

REPENTANCE 111

REPUTATION 111

REVENGE...111

REVOLUTION..111

REWARD 112

RICHES 112

RIGHT 112

RISE 113

CHAPTER NINETEEN......................114

SACRIFICE..114

SATAN 114

SCIENCE 114

SECURITY...114

SECRET 115

SEED..115

SELF...115

SILENCE 115

SIMPLICITY 115

SINNER 116

SOLUTION 116

SOUL 116

SPEECH..116

STRUGGLE 117
STUPIDITY 117
SUCCESS 117
SUFFERING 118
SURVIVAL 119
SYSTEM 119

CHAPTER TWENTY 120

TEAM 120
TEMPTATION 120
TIME 120
THINKER 121
THINKING 121
TERRORISM 121
THOUGHT 122
TODAY 122
TRAGEDY 122
TRAILS 122
TROUBLE 122
TRUST 123
TYRANNY 123

CHAPTER TWENTY ONE 124

UNDERSTANDING 124

UPRIGHT 124

CHAPTER TWENTY-TWO..................125

VALUES 125

VANITY 125

VIOLENCE 125

VIRTUE 125

VISION..126

CHAPTER TWENTY-THREE................129

WAR 129

WALK 129

WATER 130

WEAKNESS 130

WEALTH 131

WISDOM 131

WISE 132

WORLD...132

WOMEN 133

WORDS 133

WORK...133

WARRIORS 133

WORRY...134

WRITING 135

CHAPTER TWENTY FOUR...............136
YOU..136
REFERENCES…………………….....137

CHAPTER ONE

ABILITY

If a drop of waterfalls in a lake there is no identity. But if it falls on a leaf it shines. So choose the best place where your ability shines. Our destiny is not created by the shoes we wear, but the steps we take.

ACCOMPLISHMENT

If you take responsibility for yourself you will develop a hunger to accomplish it.

They say; old age is regret, but its sign of accomplishment for those who made proper use of their time.

Every human was created to accomplish something that no one else can accomplish. *Dr. Myles Monroe*

ACTION

The origin of action—it's efficient, not its final cause—is choice, and that of choice is desire and reasoning with a view to an end. *Aristotle*

If you want to know someone's mind, listen to their words. If you want to know their heart, watch their actions.

ADVERSITY
Adversity causes some men to break, others to break the record.

ADVICE
A fly that does not take advice. Follows the dead to the grave.

AFRAID
Be not afraid of going slowly; be afraid only of standing still. Chinese proverb

AGREEMENT
Too much agreement kills a chat.

AMBITION
None save self can raise the self.

I charge you, fly away ambition, Love yourself last; cherish those hearts that hate you. To silence envious tongues, be just, and fear not. *William Shakespeare.*

If you must move mountain tomorrow you must start lifting stone today.

A slave has but one master; an ambitious man has as many masters as there are people who may be useful in bettering his position. *Jean de La Bruyère*

Ah, but a man's reach should exceed his grasp, or what's a heaven for? *Robert Browning*

Ambition is the grand enemy of all peace. *John Cowper Powys*

Ambition, in a private man a vice.
Is in a prince the virtue. *Philip Massinger*

And he that strives to touch the stars,
Oft stumbles at a straw. *Edmund Spenser*

Ambition should be made of sterner stuff. *William Shakespeare*

Be ashamed to die until you have won some victory for humanity. *Horace Mann*

Children, you must remember something. A man without ambition is dead. A man with ambition but no love is dead. A man with ambition and love for his blessings here on earth is ever so alive. Having been alive, it won't be hard, in the end, to lie down and rest. *Pearl Bailey*

Cromwell was a man in whom ambition had not wholly suppressed, but only suspended, the sentiments of religion. *Edmund Burke*

Every calling is great when greatly pursued. *Oliver Wendell Holmes, Jr.*

Every man has a lurking wish to appear considerable in his native place. *Samuel Johnson*

Fain would I climb, yet fear I to fall. *"If thy heart fails thee, climb not at all."*
Attributed to Walter Raleigh

Get fired. If you're not pushing hard enough to get fired, you're not pushing hard enough. *Tom Peters*

Go for the moon. If you don't get it, you'll still be heading for a star. *Willis Reed*

Dreams indeed are ambition. For the very substance of the ambitious is merely the shadow of a dream. *William Shakespeare*

He does not wish to appear the best but to be it. *Aeschylus*

Don't think of the problem, but identify the problem and think of the solution. *J. Willie*

I have heard of a man who had a mind to sell his house, and therefore carried a piece of brick in his pocket, which he showed as a pattern to encourage purchasers. *Jonathan Swift*

I never wanted to be a crumb. If I had to be a crumb, I'd rather be dead. *Lucky Luciano*

If I can conceive it and believe it, I can achieve it. It's not my *ap*titude but my *att*itude that will determine my *alt*itude—with a little intestinal fortitude! *Jesse Jackson*

I've got a great ambition to die of exhaustion rather than boredom. *Angus Grossart*

Love's but the frailty of the mind.
When 'is not with ambition joined. *William Congreve*

Mama exhorted her children at every opportunity to 'jump at de sun.' We might not land on the sun, but at least we would get off the ground. *Zora Neale Hurston*

No more worlds to conquer. *Attributed to Alexander the Great*

The ripest peach is highest on the tree. *James Whitcomb Riley*

The rising unto place is laborious, and by pains, men come to greater pains; and it is sometimes base, and by indignities, men come to dignities. The standing is slippery, and the regress is either a downfall or at least an eclipse. *Francis Bacon*

There is always room at the top. *Attributed to Daniel Webster*

Well, it is known that ambition can creep as well as soar. *Edmund Burke*

Well-being and happiness never appeared to me as an absolute aim. I am even inclined to compare such moral aims to the ambitions of a pig. *Albert Einstein*

I have had to learn the simplest things last.

ANARCHISM

Anarchism is founded on the observation that since few men are wise enough to rule themselves, even fewer are wise enough to rule others.

ANGER

An angry man is always a stupid man.
   Chinua Achebe

The man who gets angry at the right things and with the right people, and in the right way and at the right time and for the right length of time, is commended. *Aristotle*

APRON

One who wears only an apron is merely tying himself with a rope. *Amos Tutuola*

ARGUMENTS

Arguments are to be avoided: they are always vulgar and often unconvincing. *Attributed to Oscar Wilde*

I love argument, I love debate. I don't expect anyone just to sit there and agree with me, that's not their job. *Margaret Thatcher*

Sir, I have found you an argument but I am not obliged to find you an understanding. *Samuel Johnson*

ART

Art will remain the most astonishing activity of mankind born out of the struggle between wisdom and madness, between dream and reality in our mind. *Magdalena Abakanowicz*

The arts then act as a reflecting mirror. The artist is like the hand that holds and moves the mirror, this way, and that way, to explore all corners of the universe. But what is reflected in the mirror depends on where the holder stands in relation to the object. *Ngugi wa Thiong'o*

ARTIST
It doesn't hurt an artist to taste a bit of madness...
Ayi Kwei Armah

ATTITUDE
When people fail to comprehend the rise of their kingdom, unfortunately, they cannot stop it when it starts crumbling. *J. Willie*

Active listening is a skill worth mastering for a successful relationship.

ATTENTION
Do stuff. Be clenched, curious. Not waiting for inspiration's shove or society's kiss on your forehead. Pay attention. It's all about paying attention. Attention is vitality. It connects you with others. It makes you eager. Stay eager. *Susan Sontag.*

CHAPTER TWO

BACHELOR
A bachelor is a man who comes to work each morning from a different direction. *Shalom Aleichem*

BALLOT
The ballot is stronger than the bullet. *Abraham Lincoln*

BEAUTY
Beauty stands in the admiration only of weak minds. *Led captive.*

Beauty is not in the face. True beauty is a light in the heart. No beauty shines brighter than that of a good heart.

BELIEVE
Believe in yourself, but do not always refuse to believe in others. *Joaquim Maria Machado de Assis*

We have always held to the hope, the belief, the conviction that there is a better life, a better world, beyond the horizon. *Franklin D. Roosevelt*

Believe that life is worth living and your belief will help create the fact. *William James*

BEST
Only the best is good enough for Africa. *James Emman Kwegyir Aggrey*

BIBLE
Prosperity is the blessing of the Old Testament, adversity is the blessing of the New. *Francis Bacon*

BIRTH
Birth counts for nothing where virtue is absent. Molière

Man alone at the very moment of his birth, cast naked upon the naked earth, does she abandon to cries and lamentations. *Pliny the Elder*

BLACK MAN
Why was it that everybody would always judge one black person by the way another black person behaved? As long as you are black, any

other black person is 'your people.' *Buchi Emecheta*

BLESSING

In terms of natural endowments, Nigerians are like a Palm tree every part of a palm tree is useful.
Bless everyone. If any refuse it, it will return to you. Curse no one otherwise, if any refuse it will return to you.

BOLDNESS

In civil business; what first? boldness; what second and third? boldness: and yet boldness is a child of ignorance and baseness. *Francis Bacon*

BOOKS

Some books are to be tasted, others to be swallowed, and some few to be chewed and digested. *Francis Bacon*

BRAVERY

I am not an Athenian or a Greek, but a citizen of the world. *Socrates*

It is better to be a human being dissatisfied than a pig satisfied; better to be Socrates dissatisfied than a fool satisfied. *John Stuart Mill*

To run away from trouble is a form of cowardice and, while it is true that the suicide braves death, he does it not for some noble object but to escape some ill. *Aristotle*

Understanding the good is fundamental, and if we hold this firm we shall have begun. If we enlarge it, we can become great; but if we regard it lightly, we shall shrivel. The potentiality of its flourishing rests with a man and no other. *Zhu Xi*

BURDEN
An old man who by himself carries one load on the head and another in his hand must have played away from his youth.

BUREAUCRACY
The concept of the 'official secret' is bureaucracy's specific invention. *Max Weber*

BUSY

Get busy living or get busy dying. *Stephen King*

CHAPTER THREE

CHAGRIN

What is chagrin to the ear is repulsive to the mind.

CHALLENGE

In the journey of life, it is not the challenges that matter but how you face the challenges.

Life does not always introduce you to the people you want to meet. But you must take steps that will lead you to the right people.

Know that challenges are inevitable in life, but defeat is optional.

The challenges we face, are to test how serious we are about achieving that which we have set out to do.

But already it is time to depart, for me to die, for you to go on living; which of us takes the better course, is concealed from anyone except God.
Socrates

The ultimate measure of a man is not where he stands in moments of comfort and convenience, but where he stands at times of challenge and controversy. *Martin Luther King, Jr.*

CHANGE

It is not the strongest of the species that survives, nor the most intelligent that survives. It is the one that is most adapted to change. *Charles Darwin.*

"Change is the law of life. And those who look only to the past or present are certain to miss the future." *John F. Kennedy*

I alone cannot change the world, but I can cast a stone across the water to create many ripples. *Mother Teresa*

If you don't like something change it; if you can't change it, change the way you think about it. *Mary Engelbreit*

The world is changed by your example, not by your opinion. *Paulo Coelho*

CHARACTER

Character is much easier kept than recovered. *Thomas Paine*

"People grow through experience if they meet life honestly and courageously. This is how the character is built." *Eleanor Roosevelt*

CHARITY

In charity, there is no excess. *Francis Bacon*

CHASE

A man that chases two rabbits catches neither. *Chinese Proverbs*

CHILD

A child becomes an adult when he realizes that he has a right not only to be right but also to be wrong. *Thomas Szasz*

A child deserves the maximum respect; if you ever have something disgraceful in mind, don't ignore your son's tender years. Juvenal

A child is a guest in the house, to be loved and respected—never possessed, since he belongs to God. J. D. Salinger

CHILDREN

A man has no children. Only women have children. So the future is theirs, while we die childless. *August Strindberg*

Children are to be won to follow liberal studies by exhortations and rational motives, and on no account to be forced thereto by whipping. *Plutarch*

Children have never been very good at listening to their elders, but they have never failed to imitate them. *James Baldwin*

Having no children had been a kind of choice up to the moment when, from a choice, it became sadness. *Bernardo Bertolucci*

It is easier for a father to have children than for children to have a real father. *Attributed to John XXIII*

It is only rarely that one can see in a little boy the promise of a man, but one can almost always see in a little girl the threat of a woman. *Attributed to Alexandre Dumas*

We don't ask people how many children they have. It is not done. Children are not goats or sheep or yams to be counted. *Flora Nwapa*

Great parents don't do things for their children but they do things with their children.

Parents who tend to dominate their children's choices eventually produce but dependent children.

There are no illegitimate children—only illegitimate parents. *Léon R. Yankwich*

CHRISTIANITY

You can never be a better person in the flesh. Only in Christ can you be good. *Chucs. O*

Before you tell me what the devil is doing, tell me first what God has done for you.

CITIZEN

If a man be gracious and courteous to strangers, it shows he is a citizen of the world. *Francis Bacon*

COLOR
All colors will agree in the dark. *Francis Bacon*

COMMITMENT
Whatever they say, most men want the woman of their choice also to be the mother of their children: a sort of visible and outward symbol of commitment and surrender. *Peter Abrahams*

COMMUNICATION
Communication is a skill that you can learn. It's like riding a bicycle or typing. If you're willing to work at it, you can rapidly improve the quality of every part of your life. *Brian Tracy*

CONFLICTS
Conflict creates room for new ideas and developmental changes. *J. Willie*

Strong families are not those which never experience conflict but successfully manage conflict when it does arise. *J. Willie*

CONSCIENCE
Labor to keep alive in your breast that little spark of celestial fire, called conscience.
George Washington

CONSOLATION
All men, somewhere, in some loneliness of their pain or of their thought, come close to God; there is no invulnerable heathen. *Martin Buber*

CONSEQUENCES
Logical consequences are the scarecrows of fools and the beacons of wise men. *T. H. Huxley*

CONTEMPT
I can tell where my own shoe pinches me; and you must not think, sir, to catch old birds with chaff. *Miguel de Cervantes*

CONTRADICTION
Doublethink means the power of holding two contradictory beliefs in one's mind simultaneously, and accepting both of them.
George Orwell

CORRUPTION

You cannot fight corruption when corruption has become a culture. Change the culture of corruption and you defeat it.

It will, I believe, be generally agreed that ERADICATION OF CORRUPTION from any society is not just a difficult task: *it is without dispute, an impossible objective. Obafemi Awolowo*

COURAGE

There is radiance in the darkness if we could but see. To be able to see this radiance, all you need do is to cultivate the courage to look. *Obafemi Awolowo*

I pray the Good Lord to give us the courage to recognize our weaknesses and to give us the wisdom to recognize the truth and, having recognized that truth, moral power to get committed to it through thick and thin. *Kenneth David Kaunda*

COWARD

196. The man dies in all who keep silent in the face of tyranny. *Wole Soyinka*

CREATIVITY

Contradictions if well understood and managed can spark off the fires of invention. Orthodoxy whether of the right or of the left is the graveyard of creativity. *Chinua Achebe*

Originality is the essence of true scholarship. Creativity is the soul of the true scholar. *Nnamdi Azikiwe*

CREDITOR

It is better to pay a creditor than to give to a friend. *Aristotle*

CROWD

A crowd is not company, and faces are but a gallery of pictures, and talk but a tinkling cymbal, where there is no love. *Francis Bacon*

CRY

Don't cry because it's over, smile because it happened. *Ludwig Jacobowski*

CHAPTER FOUR

DANCE

A dance is a measured pace, as a verse is a measured speech. *Francis Bacon*

You've gotta dance like there's nobody watching. *William W. Purkey*

DEAD

Come not, when I am dead
To drop thy foolish tears upon my grave,
To trample round my fallen head,
And vex the unhappy dust thou wouldst not save. *Alfred Tennyson*

In any country, there must be people who have to die. They are the sacrifices any nation has to make to achieve law and order. *Idi Amin*

I do not believe that any man fears to be dead, but only the stroke of death. *Francis Bacon*

At last, there is a lasting solution to the problem of this world; death.

I'm the one that's got to die when it's time for me to die, so let me live my life the way I want to. *Jimi Hendrix*

Men fear death, as children fear to go in the dark; and as that natural fear in children is increased with tales, so is the other. *Francis Bacon*

DEBT
A debt may get moldy, but it never decays. *Chinua Achebe*

DECISION
A hash decision does not always provide a desired objective but is always repulsive.

"The most difficult thing is the decision to act, the rest is merely tenacity. The fears are paper tigers. You can do anything you decide to do. You can act to change and control your life; and the procedure, the process is its own reward." *Amelia Earhart*

DEMOCRACY
Where some people are very wealthy and others have nothing the result will be either extreme democracy or absolute oligarchy, or despotism

will come from either of those excesses. *Aristotle*

DESIRE
It is vicious to give in to our desires, but not to have any desires at all is impossible for our weak nature. *Peter Abelard*

It is vicious to give in to our desires, but not to have any desires at all is impossible for our weak nature. *Peter Abelard*

DESPAIR
Despair is the one sin that cannot be forgiven. *Ngugi wa Thiong'o*

DESTINATION
You will never reach your destination if you stop and throw stones at every dog that barks.

DESTINY
Man is the architect of his destiny.

DETERMINATION
No matter how strong a cock is, it cannot be stronger than hot water.

Don't ask God to guide your footsteps if you're not willing to move your feet.

Let the West have its Technology and Asia its Mysticism! Africa's gift to world culture must be in the realm of human relationships. *Kenneth David Kaunda*

What you don't do determines what you can do. *Tim Ferriss.*

It is the question you ask that will determine your understanding.

Watch the costs and the profits will take care of themselves. *Aristotle*

DIFFICULTY

When people say they'd like to be in your shoes, it is usually after the difficult journey is finished. *Tim Fargo*

The ascent of a mountain is difficult but with guided cautions, but the descend is easy but with pitfalls.

In the middle of a difficulty lies opportunity. *Albert Einstein*

DISAPPOINTMENT

The greatest disappointment is the one that comes from self.

DISCIPLINE

Every man of destiny is a policeman of himself. He does not need to be policed before he does the right thing.

When preventing your children from going through pains of discipline, just understand that you're automatically preparing them for pains of regret in the future.

Without discipline, true freedom cannot survive. *Kwame Nkrumah*

DISCOURAGEMENT

Discouragement and failure are two of the surest stepping stones to success. *Dale Carnegie*

DISCOVERY

The greatest discovery of any generation is that a human being can alter his life by altering his attitude. *William James*

DISTRACTION

Your mind is your power. The Devil using the distraction of worry is after your mind so that you will lose your power. *T. D Jakes*

DOUBT

I wouldn't believe Hitler was dead, even if he told me so himself. *Attributed to Hjalmar Schacht*

In order to be true to one's conscience and true to God, a righteous man has no alternative but to refuse to cooperate with an evil system. *Martin Luther King, Jr.*

If a man will begin with certainties, he shall end in doubts; but if he will be content, to begin with, doubts, he shall end in certainties. *Francis Bacon*

DREAM

You need to have the right attitude to take the right action because, without action, all you have is a meaningless dream.
Before your dreams can come true, you have to have those dreams, *Dr. Joyce Brothers*

Life is meaningless without dreams. Dreams are the oil or tonic for a productive life.

God loves dreamer, He gives visions, and He is attracted to people who love to dream big. *Dr. Myles Monroe*

The poorest person in the world is a person without a dream. *Dr. Myles Monroe*

The biggest adventure you can take is to live the life of your dreams. *Oprah Winfrey*

Remember your dreams and fight for them. You must know what you want from life. There is just one thing that makes your dream become impossible: the fear of failure. *Paulo Coelho*

All our dreams can come true if we have the courage to pursue them. *Walt Disney*

The dreamers are the saviors of the world. *James Allen*

CHAPTER FIVE

ECONOMY
The successful economies of the future will excel at generating and disseminating knowledge, and commercially exploiting it. *Tony Blair*

EDUCATION
The roots of education are bitter, but the fruit is sweet. *Aristotle*

Education is not the learning of Facts. It's Rather the training of the mind to think.

There is no education like adversity. *Benjamin Disraeli*

ELDER
When an elder is dancing, it is an ovation that tells him when he is doing well.

ELECTION
Election: A swarm of high and low agents of the Government falls on villages and towns and unfolds the whole repertory of its overbearing acts, puts in practice all the arts of abuse, and

realizes the most outrageous falsifications and manipulations and tries on the most ingenious tricks and deceits. *Antonio Maura*

EMOTION

Emotion remains elusive when not properly conceived by the mind.

Emotion, if used positively, can be a good weapon to succeed.

ENEMY

I destroy my enemy when I make him a friend. *Abraham Lincoln*

ENDURANCE

The manner in which one endures what must be endured is more important than the thing that must be endured. *Dean Acheson*

ENGLAND

481. In England you worship two goddesses; one is Christmas, the other one is holidays. As soon as they finish advertising for Christmas on television and in the papers, the next big thing is the annual holiday. *Buchi Emecheta*

ENVIRONMENT

The environment is man's first right. Without a safe environment, man cannot exist to claim other rights, be they political, social, or economic. *Ken Saro-Wiwa*

EQUALITY

A good many observers have remarked that if equality could come at once the Negro would not be ready for it. I submit that the white American is even more unprepared. *Martin Luther King, Jr.*

EQUITY

He who goes to equity must go with clean hands.

EUROPE.

The whole world is covered over with the hell of Europe. *Ayi Kwei Armah*

EVIL

Evil denotes the absence of Good. But it is not every absence of good that is called evil. *Thomas Aquinas*

Good can imagine Evil, but Evil cannot imagine Good. *W. H. Auden*

To ignore evil is to become, accomplice to it.
MLK

EXCLUSION
Peace cannot be built on exclusion. *Gerry Adams*

EXCELLENCE
"The quality of a person's life is in direct proportion to their commitment to excellence, regardless of their chosen field of endeavor." Vince Lombardi

CHAPTER SIX

FAITH
Faith means acting or doing or working in line with what you believe. Faith and work are inseparable

FALSEHOOD
Those who lead with falsehood are doomed to live with it all their life.

FAME
Fame is like a river that beareth up things light and swollen and drowns things weighty and solid. *Francis Bacon*

FAMILY
I think the family is the place where the most ridiculous and least respectable things in the world go on. *Ugo Betti*

FATE
Accept the thing that fate binds you, and love the people which fate brings you together, but do so with all your heart. *Marcus Aurelius*.

FEAR
Optimism fades as fear rises.

The terrible thing is that those who fear are always in the majority. Bessie Head

FLATTER
A fool flatters himself; a wise man flatters the fool. *Edward G.B*

FOCUS
He who passively accepts evil is as much involved in it as he who helps to perpetrate it. *Martin Luther King, Jr.*

The man who creeps forward inch by inch may well arrive at his destination when the man who jumps without being able to see the other side may well fall and cripple himself. *Julius Kambarage Nyerere*

Socrates declared that he knew nothing, except the fact of his ignorance. *Diogenes Laërtius*

FOOLS
Why should we always imagine others to be Fools, Just because they love us? *Ama Ata Aidoo*

FOOTPRINT
Lives of great men all remind us that we can make our lives sublime, departing leave behind us, footprints at the sands of time.

FORGIVENESS
'We read that we ought to forgive our enemies, but we do not read that we ought to forgive our friends.' *Francis Bacon*

Always forgive your enemies—but never forget their names. *Attributed to Robert Kennedy*

FRIENDS
Don't waste your tears when fake friends say goodbye.

A friend in power is a friend lost. *Henry Adams*

I've not always been steady in my pursuits but my undying desire is for everyone to become friends to my best friend, Jesus Christ.

FRUSTRATION
A frustrated man will look for the nearest tree to hang himself but a frustrated woman will look for the neck of the nearest man to hang herself.

FULFILLMENT

Fulfillment grows in the power of silence.

CHAPTER SEVEN

GAIN
For everything you have missed, you have gained something else, and for everything you gain, you lose something else. *Ralph Waldo Emerson*

GIFT
Your gift will make a way for you in the world and enable you to fulfill your vision. *Dr. Myles Monroe*

GIRLS
Good girls go to heaven, bad girls go everywhere. *Attributed to Helen Gurley Brown*

GIVING
No one has ever become poor by giving. *Anne Frank*

GOALS
Those who set financial goals with clear deadlines often end up having their goals achieved.

Not having a specific and practical plan towards achieving your goals is as good as not setting the goals at all.

My philosophy of life is that if we make up our mind what we are going to make of our lives, then work hard toward that goal, we never lose--somehow we win out. Ronald Reagan

If you want to live a happy life, tie it to a goal, not to people or things. *Albert Einstein*

GOD

God completed you before He created you. *Dr. Myles Monroe*

God created everything and everyone with a purpose. *Dr. Myles Monroe*

God Almighty first planted a garden. And indeed it is the purest of human pleasures. *Francis Bacon*

It was better to have no opinion of God at all, than such an opinion as is unworthy of him. *Francis Bacon*

Where God hath a temple, the Devil will have a chapel. *Robert Burton*

Dear God, please don't let me make a fool of myself tonight. Tallulah Bankhead

GOOD
Good intentions can be evil, Both hands can full of grease. You know that sometimes Satan comes as a man of peace. *Bob Dylan*

We call the intention good which is right in itself, but the action is good, not because it contains within it some good, but because it issued from a good intention. *Peter Abelard* \

There are good women and good men but they seldom join their lives together. *Bessie Head*

GOOD PERSON
When you see a GOOD PERSON think of becoming like Him or Her. When you see someone NOT GOOD, REFLECT on your own weak points. *Confucius*

GOVERNANCE

The very ridiculous matter in this 21st-century modern world, we have allowed ourselves to be governed by murderers and cultists, ritualist and looters of public funds.

We prefer self-government with danger to servitude in tranquility. *Kwame Nkrumah*

No man is good enough to govern another man without that other's consent. *Abraham Lincoln*

The danger is not that a particular class is unfit to govern. Every class is unfit to govern. *Lord Acton*

That form of government is best in which every man, whoever he is, can act best and live happily. *Aristotle*

GREATEST

The greatest gift you can give to someone is your TIME. Because when you give your time, you are giving a portion of your life that you will never get back.

GROWTH

Growth in life means losing outdated ideas and acquiring new genuine ones,

CHAPTER EIGHT

HAPPINESS

You must learn to ignore and overlook many things if you truly want happiness in life.

The secret of happiness, you see, is not found in seeking more, but in developing the capacity to enjoy less. *Socrates*.

The happiness of your life depends upon the quality of your thought. *Marcus Aurelius*

Our greatest happiness does not depend on the condition of life in which chance has placed us, but is always the result of a good conscience, good health, occupation, and freedom in all just pursuits. *Thomas Jefferson*

Be happy for this moment. This moment is your life. Omar Khayyam

Very little is needed to make a happy life; it is all within yourself, in your way of thinking. *Marcus Aurelius*

HARMONY
You can play a tune of sorts on the white keys, and you can play a tune of sorts on the black keys, but for harmony, you must use both the black and the white. *James Emman Kwegyir Aggrey*

HATE
Hateful to me as the gate of hell is he who speaks one thing with his lips but hides another in his heart.

It is better to be hated for what you are than to be loved for what you are not. *Andre Gide*

HEALTH
A healthy body is the guest-chamber of the soul, a sick its prison. *Francis Bacon*

HEART
Certain things catch your eye, but pursue only those that capture the heart. *India Proverb*

The heart, like the stomach, wants a varied diet. *Gustave Flaubert*

HOLD ON

Hold on to what is good, if it is a handful of dirt. Hold on to what you believe, even if it is a tree that stands by itself. Hold on to what you must do, even if it is a long way from here. Hold on to life, even if it easier to let go. Hold on to my hand, even if I have gone away from you.

HONESTY

Honesty is an expensive gift, don't expect it from cheap people.

Honor

Content thyself to be obscurely good. When vice prevails, and impious men bear sway, the post of honor is a private station. *Joseph Addison*

HOPE

Hope is the last to abandon the unhappy.

When hope dies, what else lives? *Ama Ata Aidoo*

The purpose of life is to believe, to hope, and to strive. *Indira Gandhi*

Hope is the bread of the poor. *Turkish proverb*

HUMBLE

The higher we are placed, the more humbly we should walk. *Cicero*

CHAPTER NINE

IDEA
The solution to every problem is locked in an idea. You can give birth to ideas by training your mind.

If only our eyes saw souls instead of bodies, how very different our ideals of beauty would be.

IMMORALITY
Immorality erodes morality.

IMPERIALISM
If Kuwait and Saudi Arabia sold bananas or oranges, the Americans would not go there. They are there because Kuwait is an oil monarchy. *Julius Kambarage Nyerere*

IMPOSITION
Do not impose your opinion, vision or influence on others for selfish reasons. Everyone is titled to his own opinion in life.

IMPOSSIBILITY
Probable impossibilities are to be preferred to improbable possibilities. *Aristotle*

The only impossible journey is the one you never begin. *Anthony Robbins*

INCOMPETENCY
Do not make excuses for your incompetence. Work on your weakness or you will drown in your excuses.

INDEPENDENCE
Never in the history of the world has an alien ruler granted self-rule to a people on a silver platter. *Kwame Nkrumah*

INFALLIBLE
The Negro is not free. He is not free at any level of living. But the fact that he is not free does not make him morally infallible. *Peter Abrahams*

INFERIORITY
Men of all senses in all ages abhor those customs which treat us only as of the vassals of your sex. *Abigail Adams*

INDULGENCE
The attitude you display when you are working for someone else's business will follow you when you finally get to work your own business.

INJUSTICE
We will not support injustice and discrimination in the name of national identity.

Injustice anywhere is a threat to justice everywhere. *Martin Luther King, Jr.*

We are out to defeat injustice and not white persons who may be unjust. Martin *Luther King, Jr.*

INNOCENT
Cockroach can never be innocent in the gathering of fowls.

INSPIRATION
Inspirations come from the deep of the heart.

INSANE
I tell you, in this world being a little crazy helps to keep you sane. *Zsa Zsa Gabor*

INTEGRITY

Your class determines your value in the society but your behavior determines your integrity.

In order to be true to one's conscience and true to God, a righteous man has no alternative but to refuse to cooperate with an evil system. *Martin Luther King, Jr.*

From any point of view, I had rather be what I am, a member of the Negro race, than be able to claim membership with the most favored of any other race. *Booker T. Washington*

INTELLECTUAL

Intellectual slavery masquerading as sophistication is the worst form of slavery. *Ngugi wa Thiong'o*

INTENTION

We call the intention good which is right in itself, but the action is good, not because it contains within it some good, but because it issued from a good intention. *Peter Abelard*

CHAPTER TEN

JOURNEY

We have to realize that we are the principal factor in determining how far we can go on the journey of life.

JUSTICES

I can answer but for three things: a firm belief in the justice of our cause, close attention in the prosecution of it, and the strictest integrity.
George Washington

CHAPTER ELVEN

KIND WORDS

Kind words can be short and easy to speak, but their echoes are truly endless. *Mother Teresa*

KINGDOM

A kingdom without a king is a fail state.

KNOWLEDGE

Knowledge gives power but character gives respect.

If we do not plant knowledge when we are young, it will not give us shade when we are old. *Lord Chesterfield*

To generalize is to be an idiot. To particularize is the lone merit of decision. General knowledge is those idiots possess.

If you dissemble sometimes your knowledge of that you are thought to know, you shall be thought, another time, to know that you know not. *Francis Bacon*

Knowledge is more important than resources.

We know what we are, but know not what we may be. *William Shakespeare*

Knowledge is knowing what to say wisdom is knowing when to say it.

CHAPTER TWELVE

LANGUAGE

The only living language is the language in which we think and have our being. *Antonio Machado*

LAW

When the law is stupid, it need to be broken. *Kenneth Kaunda.*

Imperialism knows no law beyond its own interests. *Kwame Nkrumah*

It may be true that the law cannot make a man love me, but it can keep him from lynching me, and I think that's pretty important. *Martin Luther King, Jr.*

The old law of an eye for an eye leaves everybody blind. *Attributed to Martin Luther King, Jr*

Law is a form of order and good law must necessarily mean good order. *Aristotle*

One with the law is a majority. *Calvin Coolidge*

LAZZY

The lazier a person is, the more things he needs to do tomorrow.

LEADERSHIP

Successful leadership is not dependent on the possession of a single universal pattern of inborn traits and abilities. *Douglas Macgregor*

A country with the right kind of leader can grow from zero to zenith in a generation

You can only be a good leader if you have a direction for the people.

Visionary leadership is important because it provides guidance that makes one effective as a leader and influential as a team controller.

A leader must have a vision and take responsibility for his vision

Leadership is not an endowment but an accomplishment.

Leadership exists in its most natural form among equals. It is not the same as domination or the exercise of power. True leaders respect the integrity of others. *John Adair*

The art of leadership is to work with the natural grain of the particular wood of humanity which comes to hand. *John Adair*

LEARN

What we have to learn to do, we learn by doing. *Aristotle*

I remind myself every morning: Nothing I say this day will teach me anything. So if I'm going to learn, I must do it by listening. *Larry King*

Anyone who stops learning is old, whether at twenty or eighty. Anyone who keeps learning stays young. The greatest thing in life is to keep your mind young." *Henry Ford*

LEGACY

Legacy is superior to possession.

Your legacy should be that you made it better than it was when you got it.

LESSON

Do not let your past determine who you are, but let it be a lesson to bring you out who you want to be.

LIFE

When you lose, don't lose the lesson. *Dalai Lama*

Learn by studying the masters—not their pupils. *Niels Henrik Abel*

Many people fail in life because they are doing things simply because others are doing them.

Life is sweet as a good melody only the lyrics can messed it up.

Start building habits for the future. If life gets in the way, don't worry. Stay flexible but focused.

You seem to have no real purpose in life and won't realize at the age of twenty-two that for a man life means work and hard work if you mean to succeed. *Jennie Churchill*

It is impossible for man to solve the riddles of the universe, as it is impossible for mosquito to bite through an iron bar.

You might not be able to control what life might throw at you, but you can control how you react towards it.

When we make intentional decisions about our goals, our attitudes about life begins to change as well.

The business of life can make us self-focused, but with a little effort, we can befriend those around us.

Your mind will answer most questions if you learn to relax and wait for the answer. *William S. Burroughs.*

Occupy your mind with what you want more of in your life.

Open your eyes and look within. Are you satisfied with the life you're living? *Bob Marley*

Detoxify your life of negative influence.

That I love, I cherish. That I hate I despair. The rest is dross.

Concern yourself with what really matters

Concern yourself with what really matters.

Life is the most difficult exam. Many people fail because they try to copy others, not realizing that everyone has a different question paper.

The unexamined life is not worth living.

In life, you will always be remembered for the problem you created or the problem you solved.

You cannot afford to remain passive or docile and expect success in life. Give your life a sense of purpose.

If you have a negative perception of yourself, you will not respect yourself.

Stop trying to rewind a life because life is not a movie.

Nothing in life is to be feared, it is only to be understood.

People are relegated in life when their thinking is delegated

Know that the beauty of the morning is not the sunrise, but the thought that God has given us another to see through life.

Life is like a dream for wise, a game for the fool, a comedy for the rich, a tragedy for the poor. *Shalom Aleichem*

No matter how bad things get you to go on living, even if it kills you. *Shalom Aleichem*

One fact in life: there will always be lesser and greater persons than yourself.

Sometimes, there are things more important than money. Be someone reason to smile.

A moment's insight is sometimes worth a life's experience. *Oliver Wendell Holmes*

If whoever created us gave us too much capacity for sorrow, He had, at the same time, built laughter into us to make life somewhat possible. *Ama Ata Aidoo*

Work like you don't need the money. Love like you've never been hurt. Dance like nobody's watching. *Satchel Paige*

LIFE'S THEORY
 When flood comes the fish eats Ants. But when water dries the Ant eats Fish. Life gives a chance to everyone. Just have to wait for our turn.

It's not what happens to you that determines how far you will go in life; it is how you handle what happens to you

In the end, it's not the years in your life that count. It's the life in your years. *Abraham Lincoln*

The greatest day in your life and mine is when we take total responsibility for our attitudes. That's the day we truly grow up. *John C. Maxwell*

Life is not a problem to be solved, but a reality to be experienced. *Soren Kierkegaard*

What we think determines what happens to us, so if we want to change our lives, we need to stretch our minds. *Wayne Dyer*

Life is ten percent what happens to you and ninety percent how you respond to it. *Lou Holtz*

Believe that life is worth living and your belief will help create the fact. *William James*

The only disability in life is a bad attitude. *Scott Hamilton*

Too often we underestimate the power of a touch, a smile, a kind word, a listening ear, an honest compliment, or the smallest act of caring, all of which have the potential to turn a life around. *Leo Buscaglia*

Life isn't about finding yourself. Life is about creating yourself. *George Bernard Shaw*

There is more to life than increasing its speed. *Mahatma Gandhi*

Our prime purpose in this life is to help others. And if you can't help them, at least don't hurt them. *Dalai Lama*

There are three constants in life...change, choice, and principles. *Stephen Covey*

Life's most persistent and urgent question is, 'What are you doing for others? *Martin Luther King, Jr.*

Life is a series of natural and spontaneous changes. Don't resist them--that only creates sorrow. Let reality be reality. Let things flow naturally forward in whatever way they like. *Lao Tzu*

Only a life lived for others is a life worthwhile. *Albert Einstein*

When life is too easy for us, we must beware or we may not be ready to meet the blows which sooner or later come to everyone, rich or poor. *Eleanor Roosevelt*

"God gave us the gift of life; it is up to us to give ourselves the gift of living well." *Voltaire*

All life is an experiment. The more experiments you make the better. *Ralph Waldo Emerson*

Once you say you're going to settle for second, that's what happens to you in life. *John F. Kennedy*

There is no passion to be found playing small-- in settling for a life that is less than the one you are capable of living. *Nelson Mandela*

If you don't design your own life plan, chances are you'll fall into someone else's plan. And guess what they have planned for you? Not much. *Jim Rohn*

In three words I can sum up everything I've learned about life: it goes on. *Robert Frost*

Life is a daring adventure or nothing at all. *Helen Keller*

Don't take life too seriously. You'll never get out of it alive. *Elbert Hubbard*

Each person must live their life as a model for others. *Rosa Parks*

Life is not about how fast you run or how high you climb, but how well your ounce. *Vivian Komori*

Transformation is a process, and as life happens there are tons of ups and downs. It's a journey of discovery--there are moments on mountaintops and moments in deep valleys of despair. *Rick Warren*

Live life to the fullest, and focus on the positive. *Matt Cameron*

My life is my message. *Mahatma Gandhi*

Not how long, but how well you have lived is the main thing. *Seneca*

In the end, it's not the years in your life that count. It's the life in your years. *Abraham Lincoln*

Do not take life too seriously. You will never get out of it alive. *Elbert Hubbard*

Lighten up, just enjoy life, smile more, laugh more, and don't get so worked up about things. *Kenneth Branagh*

The trick in life is learning how to deal with it. *Helen Mirren*

Anyone who lives within their means suffers from a lack of imagination. *Oscar Wilde*

Life can only be understood backward, but it must be lived forwards. *Soren Kierkegaard*

Life isn't about finding yourself. Life is about creating yourself. *George Bernard Shaw*

Life always waits for some crisis to occur before revealing itself at its most brilliant. *Paulo Coelho*

LIBERALS

Sadly I have come to realize that a great many so-called liberals aren't liberal they will defend to the death your right to agree with them. *Ronald Reagan*

When a liberal is abused, he says: Thank God they didn't beat me. When he is beaten, he thanks God they didn't kill him. When he is killed, he will thank God that his immortal soul has been delivered from its mortal clay. *Vladimir Ilyich Lenin*

LIGHT

Stop, look around and realize just how many people are using your light to illuminate their path. *David Carrizales*

LITERACY

In honest hands, literacy is the surest and the most effective means to true education. In dishonest hands, it may be the most dangerous, in fact, a suicidal, acquisition. *Obafemi Awolowo*

LITERATURE

Literature is the honey of a nation's soul, preserved for her children to taste forever, a little at a time! *Ngugi wa Thiong'o*

"Literature adds to reality, it does not simply describe it. It enriches the necessary competencies that daily life requires and provides; and in this respect, it irrigates the deserts that our lives have already become." *C. S. Lewis*

LIVING

"We make a living by what we get, but we make a life by what we give." *Winston Churchill*

LONELINESS

Loneliness does not come from having any people around you. But from being unable to communicate the things that seem important to you. *Carl Jung*

LOVE

Love: The eyes of a lover tell lies. *Peter Abrahams*

Why should I be angry with a man for loving himself better than me? *Francis Bacon*

Love is composed of a single soul inhabiting two bodies. *Aristotle*

Darkness cannot drive out darkness; only light can do that. Hate cannot drive out hate; only love can do that. *Martin Luther King*

It is preferable to change the world on the basis of the love of mankind. But if that quality is too rare, then common sense seems the next best thing. *Bessie Head*

Love must be free as the wind; it must not be chained nor used as a wedge to make unnecessary demands.

Loving atmosphere in your home is like the foundation for your life.

Love the life you live. Live the life you love. *Bob Marley*

Love all, trust a few, do wrong to none. *William Shakespeare*

The greatest pleasure of life is love. *Euripides*

CHAPTER THIF

MADNESS

'Mad' is a term we use to d
obsessed with one idea ar
Betti

MAN

A good man can be stupid and still be good. But a bad man must have brains. *Maksim Gorky*

Real men don't follow the title but follow courage.

The true measure of a man is not where he stands in the moment of comfort and convenience but in the time of challenge and controversy. *Martine Luther*.

A noisy man is always in the right. *William Cowper*

Men come of age at sixty, women at fifteen. *James Stephens*

Man, that is born of a woman hath but a short time to live and is full of misery. *Book of Common Prayer*

y, oh why, do I always trust men, look up to them more than to people of my own sex, even though I was brought up by women? *Buchi Emecheta*

A man's greatest battles are the ones he fights within himself. *Ben Okri*

A superior man is modest in his speech but exceeds in his action. *Confucius*

No man is more hated than he who speaks the truth. *Plato*

MANIPULATION
If the means you employ to motivate others are hidden from them or seek to bypass their conscious minds, then one is becoming a manipulator rather than a motivator. *John Adair*

MARRIAGE
Nearly all the failures married white women. Maybe it was the only way of boosting their egos, or was it a way of getting even with their colonial masters? *Buchi Emecheta*

Our people say a bad marriage kills the soul. Mine is fit for burial. *Ama Ata Aidoo*

Your experience will be a lesson to all of us men to be careful not to marry ladies in very high positions. *Idi Amin*

MAJORITY
The one pervading evil of democracy is the tyranny of the majority. *Lord Acton*

MASSES
Religion is the opium of the masses. *Karl Max*

MEDIA
The media has a way of launching public figures into the stratosphere and then yanking them back to earth without a parachute. *Howard Kurtz*

MEETING
We meet to discuss our plans, voice out opinions and air out our grievances; these are the essentials of a meeting.

MEMORANDUM
A memorandum is written not to inform the reader but to protect the writer. *Dean Acheson*

MEMORIES
Memories are like stones, time and distance erode them like acid. *Ugo Betti*

MEN
Men are good in one way, but bad in many. *Aristotle*

MERIT
My experience is that there is something in human nature that always makes an individual recognize and reward merit, no matter under what color of skin merit is found. *Booker T. Washington*

MISSION
"My mission in life is not merely to survive, but to thrive; and to do so with some passion, some compassion, some humor, and some style." *Maya Angelou*

MISTAKE
A man who makes no mistakes does not usually make anything. Making mistakes is better than faking perfection.

Mistake to a positives guided man actualizes to success at the end.

The greatest mistake I ever made was not to die in office. *Attributed to Dean Acheson*

Each life is made up of mistakes and learning, waiting and growing, practicing patience and being persistent. *Billy Graham*

MIRACLES

Miracles are instantaneous, they cannot be summoned, but come of themselves, usually at unlikely moments and to those who least expect them. *Katherine Anne Porter*

MISERABLE

So long as men worship the Caesars and Napoleons, Caesars and Napoleons will arise to make them miserable. *Aldous Huxle*

MONEY

Only when the last tree has died and the last river been poison and the last fish been caught will we realize we cannot eat money. *India proverb*

MOTION

The motion being eternal, the first mover, if there is but one will be eternal also. *Aristotle*

When the present is intolerable, the unknown Harbours no risks. *Wole Soyinka*

MOTIVATION

Life takes on meaning when you become motivated, set goals and charge after them in an unstoppable manner. *Les Brown*

MUSIC

Music has the power of producing a certain effect on the moral character of the soul, and if it has the power to do this, it is clear that the young must be directed to music and must be educated in it. *Aristotle*

Life is like playing a violin in public and learning the instrument as one goes on. *Samuel Butler*

CHAPTER FOURTEEN

NATURE
Look deep into nature, and then you will understand everything better. *Albert Einstein*

NECESSITY
If necessity is the mother of invention, the recession is the father of consciousness. *Anon*
Until someone realizes his need for God he will not reach out to God to save him.

NOTHING
Nothing haunts us like the things we don't say. *Mitch Albom*

CHAPTER FIFTEEN

OLD

It is so surprising, is it not, how even the worst happenings of the past acquire a sweetness in the memory. Old harsh distresses are now merely pictures and tastes which hurt no more, like itching scars which can only give pleasure now. *Ayi Kwei Armah*

Being over seventy is like being engaged in a war. All our friends are going or gone and we survive amongst the dead and the dying as on a battlefield. *Muriel Spark*

The man at 45 years is about to be placed on shelve while a woman of 35 is already on the shelve.

OLD AGE

I used to think getting old was about vanity—but actually, it's about losing people you love. *Joyce Carol Oate*

Let us take care that age does not make more wrinkles on our spirit than on our face. *Michel de Montaigne*

OPINION

Stop making other people's opinion of you more important than your own.

OPPORTUNITY

A wise man will make more opportunities than he finds. *Francis Bacon*

OBSTINATE

Obstinate people can be divided into the opinionated, the ignorant, and the boorish. *Aristotle*

OPPRESSION

Only free men can negotiate; prisoners cannot enter into contracts. *Nelson Mandela*

To overthrow oppression has been sanctioned by humanity and is the highest aspiration of every free man. *Nelson Mandela*

OPTIMISM

Perpetual optimism is a force multiplier. *Colin Powell*

CHAPTER SIXTEEN

PARADISE
Grant me paradise in this world; I'm not so sure I'll reach it in the next. *Attributed to Tintoretto*

PARTNER
A true partner is the one who cannot solve all the problems in your life but promise to face to face all of them with you.

PEOPLE
Most people don't know who they are, so they die as someone else. *Myles Monroe*

People are worms, and even the God who created them is immensely bored with their antics. *Ama Ata Aidoo*

The Lord prefers common-looking people. That is why he makes so many of them. *Abraham Lincoln.*

People will do anything, no matter how absurd, to avoid facing their own souls. *Carl Jung.*

To understand the true quality of people, you must look into their minds and examine their pursuits and aversions. *Marcus Aurelius*

Arguing with fools is like killing the mosquito on your cheek. You might kill it or not, but you'll end up slapping yourself for sure.

Care about what other people think and you will be their prisoner. *Lao Tzu*

PERFECTION
You would attain to the divine perfection,
and yet not turn your back upon the world.
Henry Wadsworth Longfellow

PLAN
If you don't plan for your continuous growth, you will automatically stagnate and deign to fall behind.

Life is what happens when you're busy making other plans. *John Lennon*

POLICEMEN

When policemen harass innocent citizens, they have reduced the dignity of their calling and abuse their office.

POLITICS

A statesman is a politician who places himself at the service of the nation. A politician is a statesman who places the nation at his service. *Georges Pompidou*

Ethnicity and religion are the banes of Nigerian politics.

Seek ye first the political kingdom and all things shall be added unto you. *Kwame Nkrumah*

The two-party systems has shown itself to be unsuitable in any African state. It has grown up in Britain to serve specific class interests. *Kwame Nkrumah.*

The battle still remains the same. It is not anti-white, but anti-wrong. *Kenneth David Kaunda*

We stand for majority rule; we don't stand for black majority rule. *Nelson Mandela*

The struggle is my life. I will continue fighting for freedom until the end of my days. *Nelson Mandela.*

Politics, as a practice, whatever its professions, has always been the systematic organization of hatreds. *Henry Adams.*

Man is by nature a political animal. *Aristotle*

POSITIVE

A positive mind creates positive ideas, a negative mind creates negative ideas and an empty mind is the playground of both.

When a negative situation arises try and be positive.

POSSIBILITY

I think everything is possible if you have the mindset and the will and desire to do it and put the time in. *Roger Clemens*

POSTULATIONS

There are in every man, at every hour, two simultaneous postulations, one towards God, the other towards Satan. *Charles Baudelaire*

POTENTIAL

If you really want to live your life to the fullest and realize your greatest potential, you must be willing to run the risk of making some people mad. People may not like what you do, people may not like how you do it, but these people are not living your life. You are.

POWER

The most awful thing about power is not that it corrupts absolutely but that it makes people so utterly boring, so predictable... *Chinua Achebe*

Power tends to corrupt, and absolute power corrupts absolutely. Great men are almost always bad men...There is no worse heresy than that the office sanctifies the holder of it. *Lord Acton*

I am more and more convinced that man is a dangerous creature and that power, whether vested in many or a few, is ever grasping, and like the grave, cries 'Give, give.' *Abigail Adams*

New nobility is but the act of power, but ancient nobility is the act of time. *Francis Bacon.*

The quest for absolute power is a gateway to dishonesty.

PRACTICE

Let us preach what we practice—let us practice what we preach.

PRAYER

God be in my head,
And in my understanding;
God be in my eyes,
And in my looking;
God be in my mouth,
And in my speaking;
God be in my heart,
And in my thinking;
God be at my end,
And at my departing. *Anonymous*

Heaven is full of answers to prayers for which no one ever bothered to ask. *Billy Graham*

Abide with me from morn till eve,
For without Thee I cannot live;
Abide with me when the night is nigh,
For without Thee I dare not die. *John Keble*

You pray for rain, you got a deal with the mud too. *Denzel Washington*

PRETENSE
We play make-believe, pretend to take ourselves and each other seriously—to love each other, hate each other—but then—it isn't true! It isn't true, we don't care at all. *Ugo Betti*

PRINCIPLES
Our empirical knowledge of fact portrays our deep reality of life.

The ethics and ethos of our society are the guiding principles of life.

PRIVILEGE
When you arise in the morning think of what a precious privilege it is to be alive, to breathe, to think, to enjoy, to love. *Marcus Aurelius*

PROBLEMS

Repair your life and stop analyzing the problems of others.

To solve a social problem, you have to create a social problem.

The best way to solve any problem is to remove its cause. *Martin Luther King, Jr.*

Until justice rolls down like waters and righteousness like a mighty stream. *Martin Luther King, Jr.*

Never let a problem to be solved becomes more important than a person to be loved. *Barbara Johnson.*

Life is essentially an endless series of problems. The solution to one problem is merely the creation of the next one. Don't hope for a life without problems. There's no such thing. Instead, hope for a life full of good problems. *Mark Manson*

To solve a problem you must have to recognize your share of responsibility. If you only blame the others, you will never solve it.

CHAPTER SEVENTEEN

QUESTION

No question is ever settled
Until it is settled right. *Ella Wheeler Wilcox*

The man who asks questions is a fool for a minute. The man, who does not ask, is a fool for life. *Confucius*

CHAPTER EIGHTEEN

RACISM
Racism: All my life had been dominated by a sign, often invisible but no less real for that, which said: RESERVED FOR EUROPEANS ONLY. *Peter Abrahams*

No white American ever thinks that any other race is wholly civilized until he wears the white man's clothes, eats the white man's food, speaks the white man's language and professes the white man's religion. *Booker T. Washington*

RECKLESSNESS
Our problem is an aged-long one where recklessness has taken the place of organized thinking.

RELATIONSHIP
The secret of a good relationship is to overlook difficulties and embrace imperfections.

To buy a possession from someone close to you passing through difficult times will be your biggest mistake you ever made. He will view it as oppression and never to forgive even if he recovers from it.

REMEMBRANCE
The remembrance of pain is always a pleasure.
Jane Austin

REPENTANCE
There's no repentance in the grave. *Isaac Watts*

REPUTATION
Associate yourself with men of good quality if you esteem your own reputation; for 'is better to be alone than in bad company.
George Washington

REVENGE
The greatest revenge is to accomplish what others say you cannot do.

REVOLUTION
Inferiors revolt in order that they may be equal and equals that they may be superior. Such is the state of mind which creates revolutions.
Aristotle

Circumstances can be changed by revolution and revolutions are brought about by men, by men who think as men of action and act as men of thought. *Kwame Nkrumah*

The gains of violence are transient; the fruits of patience are imperishable. *Kwame Nkrumah*

REWARD
The cost of doing good is high, but the reward is higher.

Socrates said, 'Bad men live that they may eat and drink, whereas good men eat and drink that they may live.' *Plutarch*

RICHES
You are not truly rich if you allow your riches to control you.

To be rich is not what you have in your bank account, but what you have in your heart.

The rich swell up with pride, the poor from hunger. *Shalom Aleichem*

RIGHT
If you are not excited about it, it's not the right path. *Abraham Hicks*

RISE

Rise above the storm and you will find the sunshine. Mario Fernandez

CHAPTER NINETEEN

SACRIFICE
When bad men combine, the good must associate; else they will fall one by one, an unpitied sacrifice in a contemptible struggle. *Edmund Burke*

Be willing to sacrifice what you think you have today for the life that you want tomorrow. *Neil Strauss*

SATAN
For Satan finds some mischief still
For idle hands to do. *Isaac Watts*

SCIENCE
Science will be the master of man. The engines he will have invented will be beyond his strength to control. Some day science shall have the existence of mankind in its power, and the human race commits suicide by blowing up the world. *Henry Adams*

SECURITY
Peace and security will not be achievable purely through armed force.

SECRET
The secret of success is learning how to use pain and pleasure instead of having pain and pleasure use you. If you do that, you're in control of your life. If you don't, life controls you. *Tony Robbins*

SEED
Seeds of today are tomorrow's harvest.

SELF
You must realize that the only person you are is yourself.

Tell me what I can do, not what I can't do.

Be yourself, everyone is already taken. Oscar Wilde

SILENCE
A meaningful silence is better than a meaningless word.

SIMPLICITY
Simplicity is ultimate sophistication. *Leonard da Vinci.*

SINNER
At such an hour the sinners are still in bed resting up from their sinning of the night before, so they will be in good shape for more sinning a little later on. *Damon Runyon*

SOLUTION
Talent itself takes you nowhere. It is the solution that talent proffers, that will take you everywhere.

SOUL
My feelings are too intense. I hate too bitterly, I love too exultingly, I pity too extravagantly, I hurt too painfully. We American blacks call that 'soul.' *Chester Himes*

SPEECH
Hate speech is said to be bad and punishable in Nigeria, what of actions that provokes hate speech?

It is generally better to deal with speech than by letter. *Francis Bacon*

I have discovered the secret that after climbing a great hill, one only finds that there are many more hills to climb. *Nelson Mandela*

STRUGGLE

Let there be work, bread, water and salt for all. *Nelson Mandela*

What I did that was new was to prove ... that class struggle necessarily leads to the dictatorship of the proletariat. *Karl Marx*

STUPIDITY

Nothing in the world is more dangerous than sincere ignorance and conscientious stupidity. *Martin Luther King, Jr.*

Never argue with stupid people, they will drag you down to their level and then beat you with experience. *Mark Twain*

SUCCESS

Confidence and continuous commitment in an idea lead to a high, celestial dogmatism which will always result to a success.

Don't let yourself feel that you need to have the natural gifts another person has or that only those gifts make for success.

I have learned that success is to be measured not so much by the position that one has reached in life as by the obstacles which he has had to overcome while trying to succeed. *Booker T. Washington*

Many of life's failures are people who did not realize how close they were to success when they gave up. *Thomas A. Edison*

"I've failed over and over and over again in my life and that is why I succeed." *Michael Jordan*

Success is how high you bounce when you hit bottom. *George S. Patton*

Most great people have attained their greatest success one step beyond their greatest failure. *Napoleon Hill*

SUFFERING

Some white people ought to be transformed into Negroes just for a few days, so as to feel what we feel and suffer what we suffer. *James Emman Kwegyir Aggrey*

Freedom is never voluntarily given up by the oppressor. *Martin Luther King, Jr.*

SURVIVAL

Our struggles today are the prerequisite for our survival tomorrow.

The ultimate value of life depends upon awareness and the power of contemplation rather than upon mere survival. *Aristotle*

SYSTEM

The process alone does not make a system to work; it is the process and culture of the system that makes a system work.

CHAPTER TWENTY

TEAM

One man can be a crucial ingredient on a team, but one man cannot make a team. *Abdul Jabbar*

TEMPTATION

And once the storm is over you won't remember how you made it through... you won't be the same person who walk in. that's what this storm's all about. *Haruki Murakami*

TIME

Don't wait time will never be just right. *Napoleon Hill*

One day you will wake up and there won't be any more time to do the things you've always wanted to do. Do it now. *Paulo Coelho*

Dost thou love life? Then do not squander time, for that is the stuff life is made of. *Benjamin Franklin*

Time means a lot to me because you see, I, too, am also a learner and am often lost in the joy of forever developing and simplifying. If you love life, don't waste time, for time is what life is made up of. *Bruce Lee*

Your time is limited, so don't waste it living someone else's life. Don't be trapped by dogma, which is living with the results of other people's thinking. Don't let the noise of others' opinions drown out your own inner voice. And most important, have the courage to follow your heart and intuition. *Steve Jobs*

THINKER
No poison can kill a positive thinker, and no medicine can save a negative thinker.

THINKING
Without creative thinking skills, you will be relegated to poverty in life. Therefore utilize your creative thinking.

TERRORISM
No one can terrorize a whole nation unless we are all his accomplices. *Ed Murrow*

THOUGHT
Two things to remember in life: take care of your thoughts when you are alone, and take of your words when you're with people.

TODAY
Today is life-the only life you are sure of. Make the most of today. Get interested in something. Shake yourself awake. Develop a hobby. Let the winds of enthusiasm sweep through you. Live today with gusto. *Dale Carnegie*

TRAGEDY
The real tragedy is never resolved. It goes on hopelessly forever. *Chinua Ache*

TRAILS
A gem cannot be polished without friction, nor a man perfects without trails.

TROUBLE

As you grow old, remember to grow along with all the troubles you created because you will never remember to pick them up again.

I love those who can smile in trouble. *Leonardo da Vinci*

TRUST

And let us not trust human effort alone, but humbly acknowledging the power and goodness of Almighty God, who presides over the destiny of nations, and who at all times has been revealed in our country's history, let us invoke His aid and His blessings upon our leaders. *Grover Cleveland*

TYRANNY

The only tyrannies from which men, women, and children are suffering in real life are the tyrannies of minorities. *Theodore Roosevelt*

The people always have some champion whom they set over them and nurse into greatness...This and no other is the root from which tyranny springs. *Plato*

CHAPTER TWENTY ONE

UNDERSTANDING

Finishing it is good but getting it right is better

Human salvation lies in the hands of the creatively maladjusted. *Martin Luther King, Jr.*

The ethical understanding of our problems is partly the solution to it.

Everything that irritates us about others can lead us to an understanding of ourselves. *Carl Jung*

UPRIGHT

The right of a man to stand upright like a human being in his own country comes before questions of the kind of society he will create once he has that right. *Julius Kambarage Nyerere*

CHAPTER TWENTY-TWO

VALUES

Values are the ethos guiding our daily lives. It's very worrisome that moral values are being eroded in our society.

VANITY

Vanity basically involves an unhealthy preoccupation with our appearance or image.

A vanity is a subtle form of pride. *Socrate*

VIOLENCE

Today the choice is no longer between violence and nonviolence. It is either nonviolence or nonexistence. *Martin Luther King, Jr.*

VIRTUE

Prosperity doth best discover vice, but adversity doth best discover virtue. *Francis Bacon*

Intellectual virtue owes both its birth and its growth to teaching...while moral growth comes about as a result of habit. *Aristotle*

It is the function of vice to keep virtue within reasonable bounds. *Samuel Butler*

As in nature, things move violently to their place and calmly in their place, so virtue in ambition is violent, in authority settled and calm. *Francis Bacon*

VISION

Good dream can keep you in focus and help you actualize your visions.

Cultivate the attitude of a winner. Step up and vision a new challenge and work in making it happen.

I don't need to be great to start. I need to start to be great.

Don't live under the shadows of your past. You have the power to start a new course for the future.

Spend time to create the life you want, else you end up receiving the life you don't want.

It is in the difficult moment of life that we realize who are true friends, or those that truly love us.

In life, there must be a limit to our quest for success. Most importantly never put things above people

One person with vision is greater than the passive force of ninety-nine people who are merely interested in doing or becoming something. *Dr. Myles Monroe*

As long as a person can hold on to his vision, then there is always a chance for him to move out of his present circumstance and towards the fulfillment of his purpose. *Dr. Myles Monroe*

Vision requires a vital connection with God. *Dr. Myles Monroe*

Vision is the only thing that brings true fulfillment. *Dr. Myles Monroe*

To have a vision is to have more than a mere interest in something; it is to have a real desire and passion for it. *Dr. Myles Monroe*

When you know and understand you were born to accomplish, that is a purpose. When you can see it in your mind by faith that is the vision. *Dr. Myles Monroe*

CHAPTER TWENTY-THREE

WAR

It is easy to go to war with other countries. It is not easy to comprehend the unintended consequences of that war.

There are only two persons who profit in war; the one who produce the weapon and the man who sells it.

I live in peace with men and at war with my innards. *Antonio Machado*

Climb ev'ry mountain, ford ev'ry stream, Follow ev'ry rainbow, till you find your dream. *Oscar Hammerstein II*

WALK

If you cannot find a good companion to walk with, walk alone, like an elephant roaming the jungle. It is better to be alone than to be with those who will hinder your progress. *Buddha*

WATER

Water is the softest thing, yet it can penetrate mountains and earth. This shows clearly the principle of softness overcoming hardness. *Lao Tzu*

A lovely thing to learn from WATER: adjust yourself in every situation and in any shape... But most importantly. Find your own way to flow.

WEAKNESS

Never support two weaknesses at the same time. It's your combination sinners—your lecherous liars and your miserly drunkards—who dishonor the vices and bring them into bad repute. *Thornton Wilder*

The best anyone can do when dealing with weakness is to get as far away from it as possible. *Nikki Giovanni*

The concessions of the weak are the concessions of fear. *Edmund Burke*

I can't stand a naked light bulb, any more than I can a rude remark or a vulgar action. *Tennessee Williams*

Having the wisdom to translate ideas to action is absolutely necessary for everyone. Wisdom terminates hardship.

When you leave power, you leave with honor. But when power leaves you, it leaves you with dishonor.

Never show your weakness to the world. Because the world is much interested to play with it.

WEALTH
When the ambition of a man is chasing after money, wealth becomes elusive.

WISDOM
If a man looks sharply, and attentively, he shall see Fortune: for though she be blind, yet she is not invisible. *Francis Bacon*

A man may learn wisdom even from a foe. *Aristotle*

Wisdom comes with maturity in age.

The only true wisdom is in knowing you know nothing. *Socrates*

WISE

Be wise with speed,
A fool at forty is a fool indeed. *Edward Young*

The Errors of a Wise Man make your Rule, Rather than the Perfections of a Fool. *William Blake*

The Errors of a Wise Man make your Rule, Rather than the Perfections of a Fool. *William Blake*

THE WISE WARRIOR AVOIDS THE BATTLE. *Sun Tzu*

WORLD

Don't gain the world and lose your soul, wisdom is better than silver or gold. *Bob Marley*
To live is the rarest thing in the world. Most people exist, that is all. *Oscar Wilde*

WOMEN

God, when will you create a woman who will be fulfilled in herself, a full human being, not anybody's appendage? *Buchi Emecheta*

I am a woman and a woman in Africa. I am a daughter of Nigeria and if she is in shame, I shall stay and mourn with her in shame. *Buchi Emecheta*

WORDS

Words are the fog one has to see through. *Zen saying*

WORK

If you want to have more, you have to become more.

If you want to eat like a king, you have to work as a king

WARRIORS

Warriors are not what you think as warriors. The warrior is not someone who fights, for no one has the right to take another life. The warrior, for us, is the one who scarifies himself for the good of others. His task is to take care of the elderly, the defenseless, those who cannot provide for themselves, and above all, the children, the future of humanity. *Sitting Bull*

WORRY

If a problem is fixable, if a situation is such you can do something about it, then there is no need to worry. If it's not fixable, then there is no help in worry. There is no benefit in worry whatsoever. *Dalai Lama*

If you wish to know the heart of a man, listen to his words. *Chinese proverb.*

Married couples are well suited when both partners usually feel the need for a quarrel at the same time. *Jean Rostand*

Life's too short for worrying. *Yes, that's what worries me.*

The secret of not having worries, for me at least, is to have ideas. *Eugène Delacroix*

There is always a problem that man cannot permanently solve; that is worry.

WRITING

Against the disease of writing, one must take special precautions, since it is a dangerous and contagious disease. *Peter Abelard*

A writer is a writer, and writing is sexless. *Buchi Emecheta*

Write and risk damnation. Avoid damnation and cease to be a writer. That is the lot of the writer in a neocolonial state. *Ngugi wa Thiong'o*

Employ your time in improving yourself by other men's writings so that you shall come easily by what others have labored hard for. *Socrates*

CHAPTER TWENTY FOUR

YOU

The one thing that you have that nobody else has is you. Your voice, your mind, your story, your vision. So write and draw and build and play and dance and live as only you can. *Neil Gaiman*

There is nothing outside yourself that can ever enable you to get better, stronger, richer, quicker or smarter. Everything is within. Everything exists. Seek nothing outside yourself. *Miyamoto Musashi*

When you are wrong, admit it. When you are right, be quiet.

REFERENCES

1. *The Penguin Book of Historic Speeches.* MacArthur, Brian, ed. Penguin Books, 1996.

2. National Archives and Records Administration.

3. "*Odyssey.*" Microsoft® Encarta® 2009 [DVD]. Redmond, WA: Microsoft Corporation, 2008.

4. *The Complete Oxford Shakespeare.* Wells, Stanley, Gary Taylor, John Jowett, and William Montgomery, eds. © 1994. Reproduced by permission of Oxford University Press.

5. The Principles and Power of Vision. (2003) Dr. Myles Munroe. Publish by Whitaker House USA.

6. Douglas Macgregor (1906 - 1964) U.S. Industrial Psychologist.

7. Putman, John J. "Napoleon." National Geographic, February 1982.

8. Kenneth David Kaunda (1924 -) Zambian president, June 1975.

9. Microsoft ® Encarta ® 2009. © 1993-2008 Microsoft Corporation. All rights reserved.

10. *The Observer (London),* "Sayings of the Week"

11. James Emman Kwegyir Aggrey (1875 - 1927) Ghanaian educator. *Aggrey of Africa*

12. August Strindberg (1849 - 1912) Swedish dramatist. *The Father* (Elizabeth Sprigge (tr.))

13. Martin Luther King, Jr. (1929 - 1968) U.S. civil rights leader. Referring to the Declaration of Independence (1776).

The New York Times, Speech at civil rights march in Washington, D.C

14. 1995 Collier's Year Book.

15. Kwame Nkrumah (1909 - 1972)
    Ghanaian president.
    The Autobiography of Kwame Nkrumah

16. Christian Leadership. (2016) Jonathan I.Willie. publish by Basjos Printing Press. (Omoku)

17. The Root of Mankind's behavior (2010) Peter Uzuakpunwa. University of Port Harcourt Press.

18. The Engineer of Human Souls.Josef Skuorecky. Washinton Square Press. Published by PocketBook New York.

19. Ferrell, Robert H. *American Diplomacy: A History.* W. W. Norton & Company, 1975.

20. © *Estate of Martin Luther King, Jr.*

21 "Julius Nyerere." Microsoft® Encarta® 2009 [DVD]. Redmond, WA: Microsoft Corporation, 2008.

22. *The View From Coyaba*

23. *Anthills of the Savannah* Chinua Achebe